VIETNAM VETERANS MEMORIAL

AMERICAN LANDMARKS

Jason Cooper

The Rourke Corporation, Inc.
Vero Beach, Florida 32964

PHOTO CREDITS:
All photos © Bill Sciallo except cover © Breck P. Kent

CREATIVE SERVICES:
East Coast Studios, Merritt Island, Florida

EDITORIAL SERVICES:
Susan Albury

Library of Congress Cataloging-in-Publication Data

Cooper, Jason, 1942-
    Vietnam Veterans Memorial / by Jason Cooper
        p. cm. — (American Landmarks)
    Includes index.
    Summary: Describes the design and significance of the memorial built in
    Washington, D.C., to honor the American soldiers who served in Vietnam.
    ISBN 0-86593-549-1
    1. Vietnam Veterans Memorial (Washington, D.C.) Juvenile literature.
    [1. Vietnam Veterans Memorial (Washington, D.C.) 2. National monuments.]
    I. Title. II. Series: Cooper, Jason, 1942- American landmarks.
    DS559.83.W18C66 1999
    959.704'36—dc21   99-29411
                                                                       CIP

Printed in the USA

TABLE OF CONTENTS

Vietnam Veterans Memorial

The Vietnam Veterans Memorial was built in Washington, D.C., to honor the U.S. soldiers who served in Vietnam.

Vietnam is a small country in Southeast Asia. Between 1957 and 1973 about three million Americans served there during the Vietnam War. Many of them did not come home.

The memorial in the nation's capital remembers the 58,132 Americans who died or disappeared in Vietnam.

Dawn lights up the Wall at the Vietnam Veterans Memorial in Washington, D.C. The Washington Monument stands in the distance.

Their names are **engraved** (in GRAVD), or cut, into a shiny, two-part black granite wall. The 10-foot (3-meter) high wall is the heart of the memorial. It was **dedicated** (DEH duh kayt id) on November 13, 1982.

The memorial also includes a **sculpture** (SKULP chur), or carving, of three soldiers and a 60-foot (18.3-meter) flag staff.

The life-sized sculpture was designed by Frederick Hart. It was put in place in the fall of 1984.

The memorial is simple in its design but powerful in its meaning. People who visit "the Wall" do not forget their experience.

Memorials lie at the feet of Frederick Hart's life-size sculpture of American soldiers.

THE WALL

The Wall is actually two walls. Each is nearly 247 feet (75 meters) long. They meet to form a shallow V shape.

The walls are made of polished black granite. Like mirrors, the walls reflect people, lawns, and trees.

Next to each name on the walls is a symbol. A diamond symbol means the person is known to have died. A cross means the person is missing in Vietnam. About 1,300 names are marked with crosses.

Somewhere on the Wall is the name of each U.S. serviceman or servicewoman who died or disappeared in Vietnam.

THE VIETNAM WAR

Several hundred Americans were sent to South Vietnam in the late 1950s and early 1960s. Their job was to teach the South Vietnamese how to defend themselves against the **communist** (KAHM yuh nist) North Vietnamese. The United States did not want South Vietnam to be taken over by the communist government of the north.

North Vietnam wanted one Vietnamese nation. Fighting between the two Vietnams grew fiercer. President Lyndon Johnson was afraid South Vietnam would be defeated. In 1965 he sent thousands of American soldiers to fight in South Vietnam.

Three comrades-in-arms stand together in the quiet, cool stillness of a winter dawn in Washington.

A boy makes a rubbing by holding paper against an engraved name on the Wall and rubbing a pencil over it.

Thousands of people, often with the help of National Park Service Rangers, make rubbings of loved ones' names.

The Americans fought North Vietnamese soldiers and the Viet Cong. The Viet Cong were South Vietnamese who hated the South Vietnamese government. U.S. soldiers could not always tell if the Vietnamese they met were friends or enemies.

By 1969, the United States had 563,000 soldiers in South Vietnam. They fought in rice fields, towns, and hot, dense jungles. Often they could not see enemy soldiers.

Thousands of men who returned from the battlefields of America's longest war suffered lasting injury.

Many Americans in the United States felt that the communists in Vietnam should be stopped. Others believed that the Vietnamese should solve their own problems. Americans were terribly divided about the war.

As public opinion turned more and more against the war, President Richard Nixon began slowly reducing the number of U.S. soldiers in Vietnam in 1969. Meanwhile, the war dragged on. Americans at home argued about the war. Americans in Vietnam continued to fight and die.

In January 1973, the United States signed an agreement with North Vietnam to stop fighting. U.S. soldiers returned, ending America's longest war.

Goldstar mothers, moms who lost a son or daughter in Vietnam, carry a wreath on Veterans Day at the Vietnam Veterans Memorial

HOMECOMING

The Vietnam War caused many hard, as well as sad, feelings among Americans. Everyone was glad the war had ended. But many felt it should never have been fought by Americans.

American soldiers returned quietly. The nation did not celebrate their return. It seemed as if America just wanted to forget the war. But the soldiers couldn't forget. They had painful memories to deal with.

Visitors to the Wall leave tokens of love in fond memory.

PLANNING A MEMORIAL

Jan Scruggs was a **corporal** (KOR prul) with the U.S. Army in Vietnam. He and many others wanted war **veterans** (VEH tuh runz) to have a memorial. A memorial, Corporal Scruggs knew, could be a public place where some of the bitterness and sadness of the war could be left. And a memorial would finally recognize the service and sacrifice of Vietnam vets.

Corporal Scruggs formed the Vietnam Veterans Memorial Fund in 1979. In 1980 the United States Congress set aside land in Constitution Gardens for the memorial.

Corporal Jan Scruggs's idea and Maya Ying Lin's design came together in the planning and design of the Vietnam Veterans Memorial.

VISITING THE MEMORIAL

Congress held a memorial design contest. The winning design was Maya Ying Lin's. Maya, of Athens, Ohio, was a 21-year-old student at Yale University.

Today, the Vietnam Veterans Memorial draws thousands of visitors and veterans each year. It has been a place for tears and a place for healing. As Maya Ying Lin thought, "The names would become the memorial."

The names have made a cold stone wall very much alive for many Americans.

GLOSSARY

communist (KAHM yuh nist) — one who supports a type of government in which personal freedoms are few

corporal (KOR prul) — one of many rankings of soldiers within the American armed forces; a noncommissioned officer

dedicate (DEH duh kayt) to honor an individual, group, or institution in a public gathering

engraved (in GRAVD) — to have been carved with letters or figures

sculpture (SKULP chur) — an artistic carving by a sculptor, one who carves

veteran (VEH tuh run) — one who has served in the country's armed forces (military)—army, navy, air force, marines, or coast guard

INDEX

FURTHER READING

Find out more about the Vietnam Veterans Memorial and the Vietnam War with these helpful books and information sites:
• Bunting, Eve. *The Wall.* Clarion, 1990.
• Devaney, John. *The Vietnam War.* Franklin Watts, 1992.
• The National Park Service on line at www.nps.gov